Clarity

A **Zellia Enjoli Tatiana** collection

Copyright © 2020 Zellia Enjoli Tatiana

All rights reserved. No part of this book may be reproduced in any form or by any means, electronic or mechanical, including photocopying, recording, or by any information storage and retrieval system, without written permission from the author. This excludes a reviewer who may quote brief passages in a review.

Cover Design: S. R. Gibbons

Published by G Publishing LLC

Library of Congress Control Number: 2019921127

ISBN: 978-1-7340865-2-2

Printed in the United States of America

Love is my religion, and in love, I believe.

Contents

- Come Close
- Say Love
- All I ever think about
- To see you
- Fruitopia
- Blind for you
- that day she let love win
- Caterpillar
- Fly Free
- An echo of its own
- Death by ecstasy
- a side order of poetry
- "cool bookbag"
- This Love
- Your Mother's Love
- Hard to get
- When love was a feeling…
- A holding pattern
- I hope you'll read this
- Used To
- Meeting
- The day I lost you
- No Light
- Heaven

- HUSSLE
- Breathless
- Air Commas
- A Spectacle…
- More Justice, More Peace

Come Close

When you touch me

it's like you touch

an off switch

on the time.

and it's not even

that it

stands still.

It just altogether ceases to matter.

What is your touch

that it causes my universe

to twirl

without confines?

And what is your touch

that it draws me to the

highest heights

of the weakest I've ever been?

When you touch me

you shift me

off center then

back into alignment again.

You send me sprawling away, weak.

Then crawling back your way for more.

When you touch me

you make doors

out of my feelings

and then open them with your smile

and

walk through them with your look.

What is your touch,

that the jones

feels everlasting?

What is your touch,

that I disarm and soften

each time you come close?

Say Love

Sometimes we ask ourselves if love is enough. The bigger part of me feels like it is… but it has to be in a language your heart can understand. We have to be loved in the ways we *need* to be (in order to <u>feel</u> it) and *then* love *is* enough. Unless love isn't what we're after, then of course, the falling and getting up and getting and staying together (in love) is surely all in (eventual, inevitable) vain.

Love is different for everyone. We give it in various ways, we receive it at varying volumes. Love is gravity. We all love uniquely, those that we love in this lifetime. Loss forces us to reflect, by default, on the power of love. We should be mindful of its power always, though.

The power of love to inspire and motivate us

to help us remember

to protect, nurture, check up on and look after us

to make us boil over with laughter

to change us, elevate us, challenge us

The power of love to name us by name

to cradle and forgive us

to add onto how beautiful, we already are…

Love is a force some will kill for…

There's a breathlessness that love can have when you let it…

Funny, but it's not, how love sometimes isn't enough. And yet love feels like all we need to be okay. Because love has sustaining *power* in that way.

All I ever think about

If I tell you

I spent

all day

thinking of you,

you will not believe me.

and so, I

say it anyway

and you catalogue it as cliché.

But I mean it.

Let me count the hours, the reasons and the ways.

All I ever think about is you.

To See You

I

want

to see you.

...

Race across your mind,

with queries endless.

For every single answer,

race back across.

Fill your palms

with these harmless

thoughts of you.

I

want

to see you.

...

Fight lightly to interpret

the prose

your pupils pour out

for me.

Wrap myself up,

loosely,

in your pure intentions.

Get far gone

off the ways you

have me in view.

I want to see you…

Discover the shallows

of your touch

and depths

of your breath.

Melt in awe,

as we kindle

and bend our souls.

Speak less and

just feel

who I see.

Fruitopia

life's simple pleasures. like good music. like flavorful food. taking my time. panoramic views of nature. creating art. thoughtful gifts… and creating them. loose leaf teas. satisfied cravings. sleepovers. the intimacy of a thing. always.

Blind for You

Loving you taught me

that

I have no idea

what love *looks* like.

I only know the

feeling.

An angel in the flesh, you are.

Leaving me speechless

about all the rest.

that day she let love win

I think of how crazy in love with me she had to be… to lean back from the driver's side of her truck to where I was sitting, on the right side, in the back seat, to kiss me.

And not once. or simply.

The kisses.

Like

she knew

no one could

see or hear us.

I think of her young son there, in the front seat. I think of how we weren't alone. And that's how I know for sure that she loved me.

Caterpillar

I'll prepare a place. A space for the recrafted me to be.

Building, even until my last drop of strength leaves me.

Fly Free

Birds do not live in cages.

They fly freely.

Neither there, are they born. In cages.

Oh, how captivity changes the song.

An echo of its own

Love has an echo of its own.

One that can travel

through

trees of forest wide

if it has to;

across

miles of ocean wide,

just to get to you.

Love has an echo

that can

find you

in a distant place,

or climbing

over mountaintops,

higher

and further.

Love's echo

permeates

captivates…

resonates

no prototype or frame of reference.

no mimicry or remixes.

no matter what, always resounding.

Love has an echo of its own.

Death by ecstasy

and just like love. everything blissful, all at once, has never been more intelligible. Never more arresting. extraordinarily, to say minimally. indefinite love. nothing but heart palpitations. having found ecstasy in you. what a way to go.

a side order of poetry

songs. music. love letters. stories. invitations. records. diaries. loss. mirrors. hopes. lies. sorrow. photographs. secrets. joys. fruit. announcements. affirmations. all parts of speech. fragment. frame. verbal. nonverbal. rumors. paintings. competitions. now. infinity. power. regrets. history books. autobiographies. coloring books. orgasms. sirens. emotions taking me over. newness. gardens. favorites. everything and all of it.

"cool bookbag"

dreams.

a fancy, backpack-full.

some of them, I am living.

more than half of the load,

I am carrying.

One by one, I pull them out, and make them become.

This Love (written at age 14)

Almost inconceivable,

this love.

Like I'm chewing on

sour starbursts.

Sweet, but shocking at the same time.

Making my taste buds

explode

with a satisfying scream.

Almost unbelievable,

this love.

Like I'm on a rising rollercoaster.

Full of surprises,

defining expectation

in this thrilling, flowing dream.

Very erotic, simply hypnotic,

this love.

I've been convicted, so I admit it, I'm addicted to

this love.

This love is bangin'.

Got me hangin' from the ceiling,

off the walls.

This love is ruthless.

Got me toothless from the sweetness

of your calls.

Almost inconceivable,

truly unbelievable,

apparently achievable…

this love.

Your Mother's Love (a Mother's Day poem)

May your mother's love

make you smile hard,

remembering how deeply

she believed in you.

May it strengthen you

to push past

feelings of frustration and defeat.

Because she was the type

to always make a way,

if one could not be found.

May it

find you

in the kitchen.

And each time

you are the hostess.

May it keep you,

as you weave in and out

of circles of friends.

When it's time

to speak your peace.

And when you're

"lockin' up shop".

May it continue to know you

intimately,

even as you age and grow.

And always love you

more than you'll ever know.

May it glow,

like a guiding light

or a lighthouse

and sow seeds of love and hope.

May it help you cope

with sudden changes.

and with what's unfair.

May it cover your beauty

like golden layers of angels cover edges of the clouds.

I pray you feel your

mother's love

today and every day.

Hard to get

She can't tell

if the bottom

will fall out of

the compliment

I just gave her.

So, she sits on it…

I'm a real one.

Gives it more of her trust

over time.

And my attention is *hard to get*.

Seeks our thread

to see if

The gold I typed

still shines.

We won't talk about

how *hard it is to keep*.

She can't tell

its karat sizes.

So, she considers biting down

on what I've said

to test it out.

Play around with my attention,

if she wants to.

She knows that what I've said is true.

When love was a feeling...

You were love

though you failed to

sometimes look it.

And

Though you

sought not to be,

more seriously.

You still were.

To watch you

turn and walk away

was the hardest thing

To do.

But then that's wrong, no.

As fast as I'd made you come

Close to me.

I knew you would move away

twice as swiftly.

The hardest part

Was knowing you

Were love

All along.

You gave me that feeling first.

You barely knew more about me

than my name

but you felt like

A cut of wind

across the baby hair

on the back of my neck.

Though

I'm sure

you weren't even trying to…

give me that feeling.

or ever trying to be…love.

And

You were, love.

You were thanks being given,

on a plate.

You were like changing lanes.

with your unparalleled intricacies.

You were.

You were good to me

and for me,

like love is.

You were love.

Though you fought to admit it.

And

Though you sought not to be,

more seriously.

You still were.

A holding pattern

waited on cloud nine

for you.

patient and

full of ideas

for what we'd do next.

waited around cloud nine

for you.

with my wings

poking through thin air.

my eyes searching

the earth below

for any sign of you.

I do not want

to land.

I don't know how much longer

I can hold still.

Here,

waiting for you.

I hope you'll read this

memories of us, in love and making it, are replaying for me. in my mind. or in my heart. I can't tell which. and I can't say that I want you back or that we need one another. if I had you for a moment, I'd say all the right things and make you feel my love for you. I'd be granted your forgiveness, without ever having to ask for it out loud. For all the times we broke up and somehow ended up together again and the former hurt you and made the latter lose its shine. for every evening and night, you told yourself "yes" and then had me. for every conversation that went left, off its intended path. you would fall back into my heart. back into my call log and threads. back in my arms. back in my life. you said you would not leave my life story. I did not know that meant you'd only stay if we were in love on all the pages. we are not in love any more.

and still, I hope you'll read this.

Used To

used to believe there is good in everyone.

used to be so sure of how I felt and what I wanted.

used to stay up all night, just to read.

used to recite other poets just to impress myself.

used to like grape or strawberry.

used to only wear white socks.

use to think that my stressing would change circumstances.

used to let fear change my mind.

used to hide my face when I cried.

used to drive east, then back west, to try and clear my head.

I used to love her…

Meeting

"pooF!"

My life fell apart in the living room.

Then the walls collapsed,

on top of my life falling apart.

Only pieces of Lalique left

and pictures of it when it felt seemingly whole.

laughing while crying.

hurting while trying.

always holding on, tighter.

And just like that.

We are fact-checking

one another's mistakes.

Shopping for bigger erasers.

Playing with our own

memory banks

like there are dials for "pause" and "play".

crying and pointing.

and trying, yet evading.

Bringing our love

and our conditions.

some of us generating it innately.

some of us mustering it up out of obligation.

the love, that is.

call it change

when hearts break.

when shelters collapse.

call it change when meeting

the reality that

things will never be the way they once were.

The day I lost you

was a word fight

that I won.

And e v e r y o n e knows

you can't stand losing.

Sad, that it's that simple.

And if it were *more than words*,

we'd probably be back together again

by now.

But our *love*

has never been more

than the word itself.

Mercy.

As I cry my last cry over losing you.

No Light

Took a shower

in the dark,

this morning.

Not even a candle.

And I've been

doing more things

without reaching

for the light first.

Which is kind of how it feels

altogether

with you gone.

Like there's no light.

And like I have no choice

but to learn to

feel my way around life again.

I need to be held

by an understanding

that swallows up

all of the ways

that I feel…

and understanding

that obliterates

all the hard parts.

life does all these wonderful things.

then backs them up with tragedy.

Heaven

You don't really think about heaven.

Until your best friend dies.

Or you see your parent cry over losing theirs.

Or you lose your parent.

Your sibling.

You lose your child.

Then heaven is just a tear away.

A night without sleep, hoping for heaven.

Then heaven is your every hope.

The ultimate dream of peace, heaven is.

Complicated, thinking about heaven is.

HUSSLE

(Ermias Joseph Asghedom, Born: August 15, 1985, Assassinated: March 31, 2019)

Humble yourself (for no one is greater than the one within you)

Understand the objective, the risks, the sacrifices and losses

See your life and its creative wingspan from a bird's eye view

Show others your true self; a mirror image of their full, potential power

Limit your excuses, complaints and your need for procrastinating

Excel by committing to generosity, philanthropy and belief in the effectiveness of a healthy community

Breathless

There is a weight to

the air I breathe.

There is a swelling

vacancy.

Grief is a cliff, with an edge too deep.

I shake my head,

but not the pain away.

My heart,

a barren field without harvest.

My mind,

a cycle of cataclysmic suffering.

My lungs,

empty over you.

I draw breaths,

and then draw more,

but not the pain away.

My lungs...

Feeling breathless, without you.

Air Commas

"It's hard to be black in America".

When they are waving their supremacy,

I am rising from my oppression

and bringing it with me.

Mine costs the human heart more agony.

The truth is

that it's "hard"

for every color.

Harder

to be black.

To just. *be.* Black.

When Black

is the reason why

this country stands at all.

Black,

demanding gratitude

in the face of discrimination.

Black,

demanding respect

as start-up-reparations.

Black.

And we will be.

No air commas needed.

A Spectacle…

we are…

and it's j u s t

her hand in my lap.

Imagine how they'd act

if we sat here, kissing.

Their eyeballs might pop out!

We should have our own reality show, the way people stare.

and it's j u s t

her

hand

in

my

lap.

More Justice, More Peace

Whose job

is it,

to come and wash all the blood away?

…

What does it

feel like

when there is no one…

and there will be no one

to come and clean

any

part

of a heart aching scene?

No one

wipes

the tears of

the mothers and fathers

the siblings and family

the lovers and friends

pleading for

more justice

and

more peace.

No one

wipes

the tears of

a neighborhood and a community

a village and a home

a people and a city

holding on for

more justice

and

more peace.

www.ingramcontent.com/pod-product-compliance
Lightning Source LLC
Chambersburg PA
CBHW031217090426
42736CB00009B/950